Large Print Sports Word Scramble Puzzle Book

Volume I: Baseball, Basketball & Football

By: Moito Publishing

www.moitopublishing.com

Large Print Sports Word Scramble Puzzle Book
Volume I: Baseball, Basketball & Football
by Moito Publishing

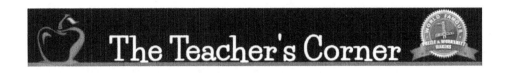
The Teacher's Corner

Word Scramble puzzles were created using the puzzle generators on
www.TheTeachersCorner.net.

Puzzles were reprinted in this book with the express written consent of The Teacher's Corner

INTRODUCTION

Study the jumbled letters and try to unscramble or rearrange the letters to form the word related to the theme of the page. Write your answer on the line to the right of the scrambled letters. Have fun!

Solutions Begin on Page 58.

Baseball Puzzle 1

1. GORHU

2. EEVRWS

3. NOPMHCAI

4. ISNWG

5. EAMYHM

6. DINVIISO

7. GDUZEORRI

8. EBRRA

9. EREJ

10. ALGUEE

11. ETASS

12. STYMES

13. ITEOCYLV

14. ERA

15. ERTHTA

16. FOIVFSNEE

17. OPTPIOTNYRU

18. EEFTGIRYCLIN

19. LEVOG

20. TIOTOMNPCEI

Baseball Puzzle 2

1. KURQI _____

2. PRTESVEPIEC _____

3. UAGRONDES _____

4. UIDIATNO _____

5. TNSRAIPAOLNII _____

6. HRIEGG _____

7. PEIOSDDL _____

8. ZNFREY _____

9. UTCLANUP _____

10. DRUEOTLFEI _____

11. BSLABLAE _____

12. TRCOREC _____

13. WROTH _____

14. OUNMATIOCMNIC _____

15. LBIEIEGL _____

16. ERFELI _____

17. BPNELUL _____

18. RRHOYWUSTTT _____

19. RPOTNOTCEI _____

20. CMSMAERIG _____

4

Baseball Puzzle 3

1. BRONSINO

_____

2. SOSA

_____

3. GDTUUO

_____

4. CEHRTCA

_____

5. OTRIYVC

_____

6. CBOB

_____

7. TEAETOING

_____

8. TOWAMRKE

_____

9. ILSNE

_____

10. NCIOITONDNIG

_____

11. HRTDI

_____

12. UNRNER

_____

13. CTTLSEAIH

_____

14. BKRCI

_____

15. ISPTERA

_____

16. NCOURNAEN

_____

17. TCIPH

_____

18. BJATIOLIUN

_____

19. DODINKASABCM

_____

20. TSMRSNPOPE

_____

Baseball Puzzle 4

1. NSAITG   _____

2. TALEP   _____

3. RIB   _____

4. DTAEPU   _____

5. TCCHEAARR   _____

6. DABEORCSOR   _____

7. TEARBT   _____

8. NTTOYROEI   _____

9. FGYEFRI   _____

10. LINNPGNA   _____

11. ETTHELA   _____

12. EOSLESSCR   _____

13. CRSHU   _____

14. TIPLLABS   _____

15. CLCETAEPS   _____

16. FULO   _____

17. CKQIU   _____

18. STHFI   _____

19. HACCO   _____

20. ALED   _____

Baseball Puzzle 5

1. LUOSEUCHB

   _____

2. RTESSS

   _____

3. MTCMOMIENT

   _____

4. ATIASMN

   _____

5. LUATBR

   _____

6. DEISLNDIB

   _____

7. PLITS-SOENDC

   _____

8. CISITTASST

   _____

9. IRCGSON

   _____

10. IUESRTVCNTI

    _____

11. HEUSLEDC

    _____

12. IGNLSE

    _____

13. UARFCTER

    _____

14. IGIRTANN

    _____

15. GUNEYRC

    _____

16. ANEEVRBLUL

    _____

17. ELSLY

    _____

18. EONTCTS

    _____

19. SUDTPEI

    _____

20. OINOTVA

    _____

Baseball Puzzle 6

1. GEAM

2. OSNMRUFI

3. LKISL

4. LITRAEETELINCOG

5. SEULMSC

6. OTHIITSLY

7. YEIRAVT

8. DEDEEBALPN

9. ENTEREEFCNRI

10. GAER

11. HSRTLSEU

12. FTBAALLS

13. NNNBGEURAIS

14. GLEIMEATTI

15. ORHNIGLEL

16. EEHRBLCSA

17. TTAAINLOIER

18. ITUETATD

19. PDRASE

20. STAANDSDR

8

Baseball Puzzle 7

1. OHWORRTVEN

2. ICSKERO

3. TIHS

4. OSLS

5. KDEC

6. ETI

7. RUICETR

8. EISSOBONS

9. RYAS

10. EMEWASO

11. EIRNIFLED

12. CRSAIHAM

13. IALVIGNT

14. YRALL

15. IETCTVADA

16. NEETMQUIP

17. NBRHOAITLIAITE

18. LDEIS

19. ERNCEXEIEP

20. RLCKSOE

9

Baseball Puzzle 8

1. FYOFLSAP

_____

2. IBALITY

_____

3. DMUNO

_____

4. EMTESE

_____

5. LSEEIINDS

_____

6. ITVNEETAT

_____

7. YTIULQA

_____

8. REECNT

_____

9. RWSDAA

_____

10. EITAMOVT

_____

11. RPEISAHELD

_____

12. AEAR

_____

13. MLBFUE

_____

14. SDTSAN

_____

15. HABARLDL

_____

16. NIW

_____

17. IOSNY

_____

18. VTICTIAY

_____

19. GEMSA

_____

20. CNEMGUETENORA

_____

Baseball Puzzle 9

1. TIRANTOO

   _____

2. AODDINM

   _____

3. BAVEULCRL

   _____

4. SCISCAL

   _____

5. ULBC

   _____

6. RPTLIE

   _____

7. ZNOE

   _____

8. SANUULU

   _____

9. SHECIT

   _____

10. APESRI

    _____

11. RIESED

    _____

12. ONSEDC

    _____

13. RKUWOTO

    _____

14. SIGTARN

    _____

15. FENSEDE

    _____

16. ANF-FTES

    _____

17. NOEWR

    _____

18. ERI

    _____

19. IWSTN

    _____

20. SENMSEI

    _____

Baseball Puzzle 10

1. PILIAMRTA

2. OPNTIEENRV

3. BOPERITDIH

4. UTO

5. EERRSBW

6. TBA

7. ATMEATEM

8. NSEMETEMARU

9. ITMT

10. ROCSE

11. REPTFEC

12. YNASKEE

13. NMEAEC

14. TIZINOAAORNG

15. AOMEITND

16. GIIWNNN

17. NAOAR

18. ESAB

19. RLBANEEOSA

20. AMNABSE

Baseball Puzzle 11

1. NEKE

2. TDARF

3. RINKPE

4. RNLSDCAIA

5. CPAEGTEREN

6. OAREEPRNMCF

7. PNELAS

8. ECEHR

9. OTOANCNNIFTOR

10. OESUTRPNISTI

11. UBCLNKKELAL

12. SEOL

13. RONGEI

14. EPEDS

15. BNLERCTAIEO

16. TNAETL

17. PCRAEAPNEA

18. IDCMAYN

19. ONRITVAIA

20. YYLATLO

Baseball Puzzle 12

1. THACC

2. TUCEEXE

3. LLA-RATS

4. EOLFUCRF

5. IRGCENTEE

6. IPMASET

7. YTTUNIAQ

8. ETKICST

9. WATRTH

10. ITFTREOUD

11. VUATL

12. IFCIFLAO

13. ACOLL

14. ERCTIHP

15. AEZL

16. TFSIR

17. ELXRMPEYA

18. OSGRDED

19. AAUCCYRC

20. ITSCIE

Baseball Puzzle 13

1. DEUGICAN

_____

2. SRAEGAEV

_____

3. ILSRIETEN

_____

4. ATICAPORPEIN

_____

5. EIOUNTACS

_____

6. COFDNENECI

_____

7. NNPPEOOT

_____

8. ESTPECENRIS

_____

9. SRATTS

_____

10. PRAYLSE

_____

11. OECFR

_____

12. UTISCGON

_____

13. ISOOIPTN

_____

14. SORTP

_____

15. AURSSITOSD

_____

16. FSLTOALB

_____

17. PTANLYE

_____

18. JYO

_____

19. ZAIGZG

_____

20. OPEHAIUR

_____

Baseball Puzzle 14

1. NWEDID

_____

2. DOMICIATEN

_____

3. ESGESVRAGI

_____

4. FLTE-AHEDNR

_____

5. PPSNSSTROMHAI

_____

6. TEAEFD

_____

7. OTRT

_____

8. LCAL

_____

9. BINHAS

_____

10. BKLA

_____

11. OSLJUP

_____

12. ELSOUZA

_____

13. OSSRSPON

_____

14. MAESCNICH

_____

15. ROUECGAUOS

_____

16. TAMCOEILB

_____

17. KLWA

_____

18. IESHLPIL

_____

19. ROUT

_____

20. PITCAM

_____

Baseball Puzzle 15

1. LRONTOC

2. RINOETPAOCO

3. AOGL

4. USBC

5. SISTENNTOC

6. SISEER

7. INEIIGBELL

8. FERILED

9. ESRD

10. ETJRE

11. KNRIAGN

12. EDIORITNC

13. TMEA

14. NNIGATUD

15. TMACMOREMEO

16. TLHMEE

17. NETLTORA

18. FEAS

19. GAT

20. UMIPCNGO

Baseball Puzzle 16

1. HOEM

2. RNASMIER

3. OTHRPTSSO

4. MTOPISMI

5. OFSEENF

6. ECUNADREN

7. NIINNG

8. ALBL

9. NBACLAE

10. TRNEI-LGEAUE

11. MNSTEAUISH

12. EPPTAROIARN

13. PMV

14. NRSOTTICUOB

15. X-YASR

16. APAPEL

17. XIAMEMZI

18. NROFCCEEEN

19. SUSITURNODI

20. YARLL-THA

Baseball Puzzle 17

1. AFNS

2. EVUOSRGI

3. ICPSMNPAIOHH

4. ORSTSA

5. ABLLERIE

6. ORSE

7. ESNPSSOOSI

8. AELTS

9. SOSEAN

10. TNDUIE

11. MLBNEI

12. FIDLIEN

13. ULSRGGE

14. TOLNSE

15. NEATBE

16. PRNIST

17. RVPNESEREECA

18. UMIORNF

19. ESMT

20. ERTOCPWONSO

Baseball Puzzle 18

1. SVSEA

   _____

2. ORUPLPA

   _____

3. NUISSTICTNRO

   _____

4. KRSETI

   _____

5. ERKJ

   _____

6. DILEF

   _____

7. DRAC

   _____

8. IBNONDG

   _____

9. ONRERSLCAVTOI

   _____

10. ADGEVANAT

    _____

11. EBULOD

    _____

12. ADACTSBOR

    _____

13. ICSDNIIPEL

    _____

14. FTIOLEUD

    _____

15. ELIVREOSD

    _____

16. FOSOISALRNPE

    _____

17. DERAWR

    _____

18. TBBOYA

    _____

19. PRKA

    _____

20. TRWHYO

    _____

Baseball Puzzle 19

1. KIRMIHSS

2. SILGNA

3. SINETEN

4. STEGRI

5. NBDOS

6. EOHRM

7. JDUEG

8. TUBN

9. MEAAGNR

10. RBSAVE

11. ELITGNID

12. MLTEAN

13. SKAETR

14. CWORSD

15. AUIDTSM

16. YHOTRP

17. RSNETGTH

18. RIEARTN

19. EEWPS

20. PRCAITCE

Baseball Puzzle 20

1. EGALLIL

2. SQDUA

3. NO-ERTHIT

4. YRAPEL

5. LAROSY

6. OMCMNO-ENSSE

7. GARNRES

8. FARI

9. EAULIFR

10. BVREIOAH

11. VECIFFTEE

12. ISTSAS

13. CTPRIIAOANPTI

14. OSELRIO

15. EGTASYRT

16. REECRA

17. LAVELUBA

18. UAGHLETR

19. AONVSBERT

20. DNIUNOB

Baseball Puzzle 21

1. OTIAUNNGTDS

2. HISNIPK

3. NRTANSGDAD

4. EMRUIP

5. AYDR

6. GRNIOCOEITN

7. NTVEROMIMEP

8. NNIADSI

9. TFROEIF

10. AVLTRE

11. INNE

12. EESSURPR

13. SEJINRIU

14. SAMY

15. GOYNU

16. THRU

17. KZIUUS

18. RNU

19. UIELNP

20. TNLOIANAS

Basketball Puzzle 1

1. SDENLESII

2. SCIITSSTTA

3. TFI

4. OTP

5. OTHS

6. THCCUL

7. CREHSTT

8. PMEECRFRONA

9. NAF

10. IMIITANAONG

11. OTPSSASOEN

12. TPACEIRC

13. LGAO

14. OSRCE

15. OPMSITMI

16. CCIRTLIA

17. JSNOONH

18. SNOIPITO

19. USSN

20. XMAMIZIE

Basketball Puzzle 2

1. RLUEARG

_____

2. PERACS

_____

3. IMTGIN

_____

4. TLAHEH

_____

5. BRDI

_____

6. OGTIORNNCIE

_____

7. ITRIPS

_____

8. SMSELUC

_____

9. IDULNVDIIA

_____

10. RCIEPE

_____

11. IUYQALT

_____

12. RANTDU

_____

13. EDBUORN

_____

14. SAPLCOEL

_____

15. NIBELESS

_____

16. RTORER

_____

17. FTVAIREO

_____

18. YRUCR

_____

19. AMGIC

_____

20. YHRYHEIOAPTSP

_____

Basketball Puzzle 3

1. SEAV

2. MLUABR

3. CLHSSRHIPAO

4. SDRCTTNEIEUR

5. NDORMA

6. ICSAARHM

7. BTRYNA

8. AYDCMNI

9. OCITAANTTR

10. IATLR

11. NRYTIASA

12. MEBUFL

13. NGETSUG

14. RHSU

15. NTOISP

16. RRITAY

17. YHAOOR

18. EOMSTRR

19. MRNANTUOTE

20. RTSEID

Basketball Puzzle 4

1. EASCR

_____

2. SIVOEPTI

_____

3. SLILK

_____

4. LOLIODWG

_____

5. AINRTRE

_____

6. ESTRNEIRTVAEPE

_____

7. RTINGIAN

_____

8. SNIRGOC

_____

9. CROORSDBAE

_____

10. SLLUB

_____

11. EUNTRVRO

_____

12. NORITNEEVP

_____

13. TTTMEPA

_____

14. RTOT

_____

15. TIEM

_____

16. ANLEL

_____

17. IEURSTMO

_____

18. PUTITAHEERC

_____

19. GFRTNALA

_____

20. SOTEV

_____

Basketball Puzzle 5

1. UMEARSE

2. SNPUISNESO

3. ETIFIDC

4. NEWIC

5. AILUCRC

6. NEFEITB

7. ERLYPA

8. NIDLIIVOAS

9. TROIYCV

10. DONAJR

11. ONITUNCF

12. IAFFCOTEI

13. TEISLCC

14. EURLLSS

15. DEGLEN

16. NSITTPSRUEOI

17. ORDWHA

18. ESAACSTSNI

19. REIGVN

20. AESTKR

Basketball Puzzle 6

1. NGSIK _____

2. EVARCLSAI _____

3. GETVAANAD _____

4. RRAGPOM _____

5. EODIRP _____

6. TEBHR _____

7. OTNTIXLAEA _____

8. IENIYTNST _____

9. LGNOIS _____

10. IRQVUE _____

11. SURDG _____

12. BTROVINIA _____

13. IAWSZDR _____

14. ASTNCACOIU _____

15. ZAJZ _____

16. MAGSMUINY _____

17. WHEIG _____

18. BYAREKL _____

19. DGRAU _____

20. STWE _____

Basketball Puzzle 7

1. NOABIIAIHRETTL

_____

2. ISNSMEE

_____

3. ECSOKTR

_____

4. HNLCCI

_____

5. AGREEECNTP

_____

6. UHOTY

_____

7. NOIMRPGIS

_____

8. QCIUK

_____

9. TINODINOIGNC

_____

10. ROTOS

_____

11. ZTLKU

_____

12. PWEOR

_____

13. GYNEICHI

_____

14. CLNEHITAC

_____

15. ATLIVOOIN

_____

16. URNYIJ

_____

17. RBILDEB

_____

18. TINAOTIVOM

_____

19. TROEBSLWMIVE

_____

20. NIICMOPETTO

_____

Basketball Puzzle 8

1. LEOMATIIINN _____

2. HRECAIMLNAB _____

3. SSERUERP _____

4. ESIINLTRE _____

5. POMIAHCN _____

6. UHRDTNE _____

7. NIISDOIV _____

8. ETAYRSTG _____

9. LSOO _____

10. IFCNEOITN _____

11. VCTOUORSII _____

12. EIHNEYG _____

13. MEMOYR _____

14. EKRNIDD _____

15. AFEETD _____

16. SMPYMSTO _____

17. SDEEENF _____

18. SGMAE _____

19. KCIP _____

20. HOPO _____

31

Basketball Puzzle 9

1. EDRLEA

2. UCOIETESCNV

3. OSNESA

4. YITLTIBAS

5. TSRAERT

6. EDRIV

7. ZEIS

8. DAINGSNT

9. OTTNPE

10. KBSATE

11. ORESNOPSIFAL

12. ADWE

13. ALNESCIP

14. KRNA

15. NAAC

16. NRGAMI

17. EMOTACLIB

18. LSERPCPI

19. PRGI

20. VESRREE

Basketball Puzzle 10

1. ANRSORETIPIP

   _____

2. XEIESCRE

   _____

3. ASCOASNTITFI

   _____

4. OMREIEVT

   _____

5. LWOJNUAO

   _____

6. MSJEA

   _____

7. INWNING

   _____

8. SVLDCAAIRUROCA

   _____

9. EZRLSAB

   _____

10. WNI

    _____

11. TGTRNSHE

    _____

12. ANDIEEDL

    _____

13. ESDASIE

    _____

14. ELAKATLBBS

    _____

15. OLSS

    _____

16. MMEEATTA

    _____

17. AITPESENL

    _____

18. IDLDPESO

    _____

19. SEBT

    _____

20. ABLL

    _____

Basketball Puzzle 11

1. ELRZZGISI

2. LNIIASFT

3. CDORER

4. LROE

5. RENCTITOPO

6. OSNESSER

7. ENGYRE

8. JMUP

9. TAIVNAL

10. IRDBNBLIG

11. TENEANTADC

12. RIRAWSRO

13. OCWRD

14. BEUNCO

15. ESZT

16. ONCRETRIITS

17. CIDIRSNOTAT

18. ENDDEF

19. TNOPISS

20. LCPIUB

Basketball Puzzle 12

1. SMITNSSAPOHPR

   _____

2. LSOE

   _____

3. NEAALCB

   _____

4. RPCETTO

   _____

5. ZROE

   _____

6. RONTIEU

   _____

7. ANNOHYT

   _____

8. IRPEWROEF

   _____

9. UEELGA

   _____

10. UDNCNA

    _____

11. LUYCK

    _____

12. SLUAUUN

    _____

13. DASQU

    _____

14. OTNTPROPYUI

    _____

15. UBTEOAKR

    _____

16. PIENPP

    _____

17. AONTIANL

    _____

18. NAEROTLIGU

    _____

19. TANDVEIILA

    _____

20. MIEOTNXEP

    _____

Basketball Puzzle 13

1. VEAIW

2. ISMTANHI

3. ZREUBZ

4. IPMIPCAOHNSH

5. NAHS

6. ZASPIMEEH

7. ASKLRE

8. USBCK

9. IEQUNU

10. ATIEMDCINO

11. YEK

12. SENOB

13. REOFC

14. NROIOMT

15. MTTIUOE

16. TICNTORAIAPIP

17. ALTYIBI

18. LEZA

19. LTHEYAH

20. CNAOUNENNMET

Basketball Puzzle 14

1. TSTE

2. GEILYNL

3. CMESHE

4. HEERBTA

5. VSAAEEGR

6. LXFE

7. VCAMRESI

8. MNROYLCA

9. KISD

10. RMAENAG

11. ITKINOZW

12. NOCRCFNEEE

13. OOCNTTKS

14. TONE

15. TWUKOOR

16. NSTAAMI

17. RCEUTRI

18. ROEUGCA

19. AEMASGS

20. PNIEOSSSOS

Basketball Puzzle 15

1. MEAT

_____

2. OTHS

_____

3. ADNREH

_____

4. NEERTC

_____

5. SNEAIPSATO

_____

6. IPNAC

_____

7. SRYTU

_____

8. RYEREOCV

_____

9. TEHSNRO

_____

10. YDBO

_____

11. ERORSR

_____

12. OTOCDR

_____

13. RKSI

_____

14. DOSIWM

_____

15. SRPUS

_____

16. MISS

_____

17. ORADABKBC

_____

18. OMAELN

_____

19. TTIAOVEM

_____

20. LISOATECUPN

_____

Basketball Puzzle 16

1. TNPIOO

_____

2. INWGE

_____

3. ETROONRBS

_____

4. IEACVT

_____

5. HCCAO

_____

6. STIITICENVN

_____

7. NSARIT

_____

8. EIT

_____

9. WHIEGTS

_____

10. NEEFSOVIF

_____

11. ATVAPEITC

_____

12. HOOSP

_____

13. EEKP

_____

14. VLAOR

_____

15. DSTGINTANUO

_____

16. LTHTAEE

_____

17. LERAETANT

_____

18. DREECNNUA

_____

19. UNDK

_____

20. RTUH

_____

Basketball Puzzle 17

1. TFAUWHCL _____

2. TETLAB _____

3. MEKFOWRRA _____

4. AVIESRGSEG _____

5. ALIHTTCSE _____

6. ORUTC _____

7. WIRST _____

8. NTSE _____

9. OTSGNR _____

10. TRPUPOS _____

11. OCLIFAIF _____

12. LEPYRXMEA _____

13. ZIIMMEIN _____

14. ECIXTIGN _____

15. FLOU _____

16. AXRLE _____

17. OTONDINCAOIR _____

18. EHTA _____

19. ETBRHA _____

20. MEGA _____

Basketball Puzzle 18

1. LOGRAEIN

2. SIKNCK

3. SSISTA

4. EOSL

5. PORASRT

6. WAHSK

7. TASNEISREC

8. ERPNIERNTTTIAO

9. RPLEEAC

10. TPINROTCEEIN

11. GJNARO

12. PAEYHRT

13. VBABILEUELNE

14. UMLPS

15. PAURCMYSE

16. GCONINCIVN

17. PYFETRI

18. DIET

19. WRKO

20. ISHATGRMN

Football Puzzle 1

1. SORSBCAR   _____

2. EALOZUS   _____

3. ASEBR   _____

4. LAGO   _____

5. ATPRETN   _____

6. PCIK   _____

7. AROLYT   _____

8. TEANBE   _____

9. EMFBUL   _____

10. MYEMAH   _____

11. YTICEOVL   _____

12. OBOSNRC   _____

13. LEBGNAS   _____

14. CALSFNO   _____

15. RUNEMBS   _____

16. FAL   _____

17. FDEATE   _____

18. UCCEBANSRE   _____

19. NITRSA   _____

20. UCHRS   _____

Football Puzzle 2

1. NITOOZNIARAG
_____

2. IMMA
_____

3. POTOSH
_____

4. MRIECSMAOLC
_____

5. CECESPLTA
_____

6. STHIIOLTY
_____

7. TSCEAHC
_____

8. COFRE
_____

9. IMEFIDLD
_____

10. ASNP
_____

11. JOGANR
_____

12. RSRGHECA
_____

13. WTEHI
_____

14. GNRDOAUES
_____

15. IMCITEOTOPN
_____

16. YJO
_____

17. AEGMS
_____

18. TOTIMEU
_____

19. NLLIEEIIGB
_____

20. EPDHIRSAEL
_____

Football Puzzle 3

1. X-YRAS _____

2. LFAH _____

3. NTOIDUNSGTA _____

4. TRAIAETIONL _____

5. IHST _____

6. EUTEECX _____

7. IOTOPPRUNYT _____

8. TEYHLHA _____

9. UUSTBK _____

10. SOOTB _____

11. ENIRHSEN _____

12. RRDOIING _____

13. IPOSSSNEOS _____

14. LAZE _____

15. RKACTABQEUR _____

16. HPTGAASUOR _____

17. QREUVI _____

18. EERCSH _____

19. DSITORSE _____

20. EILTESNIR _____

Football Puzzle 4

1. NLTVEIO _____

2. MSRA _____

3. IHTSM _____

4. NDIIISOV _____

5. OIDSPNLH _____

6. NIEPELMCOT _____

7. CIRVPTSEEEP _____

8. CECSSSU _____

9. MASACHRI _____

10. SNAREDS _____

11. EPSWE _____

12. TIAYVRE _____

13. GTLIAELCOE _____

14. BUNIDON _____

15. ECTNORGIONI _____

16. ISNPAOS _____

17. PSRTO _____

18. EYRGADA _____

19. GNVIIKS _____

20. ILLKS _____

Football Puzzle 5

1. ONAITVARI _____

2. SCRDBAOAT _____

3. GTROETHE _____

4. GIWN _____

5. AEYTPNL _____

6. OHEICDW _____

7. SCLKOER _____

8. TBINAREOHATIIL _____

9. SEROC _____

10. ROGHU _____

11. CCYCAAUR _____

12. SWBNOR _____

13. TIUCRRE _____

14. JKRE _____

15. EAAGNRM _____

16. IRE _____

17. DRNALOTTAII _____

18. IBAITYL _____

19. RECI _____

20. SLCOT _____

Football Puzzle 6

1. EEAGUL

2. RATEFRUC

3. OCENISID

4. LYIQAUF

5. LLEYS

6. CORTIYV

7. SHIRISKM

8. KIDLCEAFB

9. ERECCFEONN

10. IET

11. TEAM

12. DEN-NEZO

13. ACJNOSK

14. NAGNNIM

15. TOIANPCTIRIPA

16. ENTETIOAG

17. TGTESHNR

18. TTOL

19. UFFECROL

20. SESRTS

Football Puzzle 7

1. NNRACNUOE

2. BECAANL

3. TARRQEU

4. ERALYSP

5. RJEE

6. EEHTLTA

7. ELEXC

8. EVRESRE

9. BFUALLKC

10. AEDDTNICIO

11. HSVAEL

12. RIECDNITO

13. RITNIONETEPC

14. WGERAGS

15. REOBACCRKN

16. RNEVOTRU

17. TMVTIOAE

18. FATDR

19. ATRULB

20. TRPISI

48

Football Puzzle 8

1. SLSTEERE

2. RKETAS

3. ISNUIJER

4. RAVLI

5. NRCUGEY

6. EIPNSANXO

7. UQICK

8. LTEKCA

9. NSRTADDAS

10. LPRATOPYIU

11. SRITODAUSS

12. OGNOCTNIDINI

13. LAEDRE

14. AAILDNRSC

15. EYNZRF

16. UNRAEECND

17. PLLAEARL

18. NEMLBI

19. NOCATUI

20. ITLET

Football Puzzle 9

1. TPNU

2. SNSEAO

3. IGLHTEILM

4. FREAV

5. SUFMNRIO

6. ADATENGVA

7. RUAGAJS

8. OESFRSIANPLO

9. DEIIBLNSD

10. GHDILNO

11. DSTROSIIUUN

12. RETFNECNIEER

13. ELHM

14. RANMIO

15. UOTTCNINSRIS

16. OEBPDRITIH

17. EANRTIR

18. E94RS

19. PIGCPILN

20. IMLAECTOB

50

Football Puzzle 10

1. IINNAGTR

2. DEPO

3. NIFYTRIELECG

4. MOSS

5. DYRBA

6. RLUIUNGAA

7. AITNST

8. SSTHLRUE

9. UCTBIILYP

10. GNIWINN

11. UEERSSRP

12. CEHLNOE

13. LEIGLIBE

14. MANCEE

15. SEAGSIEGVR

16. ERNAEUSMMET

17. RNNMITIIESOS

18. ANMASTI

19. OCUSROGUAE

20. ESND

Football Puzzle 11

1. AESMOWE

2. WRIVAE

3. NLF

4. GENECPTAER

5. PAESSS

6. FDENOCIECN

7. LNEEISATP

8. TSRGINA

9. MKAEROTW

10. EVOCIEUNSTC

11. EEISONILVT

12. ITVNAOO

13. KSCAERP

14. NLUAUSU

15. TNPREENVOI

16. EPSNRTAT

17. RAEG

18. FILOFAIC

19. UITNGADN

20. ONONRINTCTFAO

Football Puzzle 12

1. UHNSRGI

2. OENFESF

3. AASDWR

4. EFRREEE

5. PITIOSON

6. DNWO

7. LLA-RSAT

8. ECDNNEAATT

9. RIGETTNIY

10. EISDARR

11. NSDNTEEMEOR

12. NSISTA

13. IUTSEPD

14. ORTCTNAC

15. SANF

16. GIAGZZ

17. ITMODANE

18. INLSEDSEI

19. AGDUR

20. NIGAST

Football Puzzle 13

1. OWDRC _____

2. OLUF _____

3. PTO-AEDTR _____

4. OTCSU _____

5. ALYEW _____

6. PRVTONMEMEI _____

7. T-NATFROIOM _____

8. LLRO-UTO _____

9. EERWITNVI _____

10. ODIVA _____

11. ZNOE _____

12. IOYRNETTO _____

13. ACMPTI _____

14. SEMSENI _____

15. SPEDE _____

16. SRGTTEAY _____

17. EAAAPRCPEN _____

18. TERCEN _____

19. AISUTN _____

20. IDAMNIRTOA _____

Football Puzzle 14

1. IKNARNG

2. IOIAEMDCTN

3. PSRTHAEN

4. LBISL

5. ISOLN

6. AHOMNIPC

7. AVNESR

8. SIEARP

9. AXEMIMIZ

10. WNORB

11. IDOSFEF

12. UOWHCTNDO

13. GRIT

14. ANOYPT

15. RCAIERR

16. FTSHI

17. UHRS

18. OCEPRTTONI

19. ISNRSDKE

20. OHYTU

Football Puzzle 15

1. WSOOYBC
_____

2. SSTO
_____

3. LRVABULENE
_____

4. EEAGSL
_____

5. EADUBLI
_____

6. ETSJ
_____

7. ILPTS-OEDCSN
_____

8. ORCDER
_____

9. IOTLCNGEEERTLIA
_____

10. TONANAM
_____

11. WRKUTOO
_____

12. SOLBW
_____

13. SSCEULM
_____

14. LUEDDH
_____

15. CPCARTEI
_____

16. BLRESCKO
_____

17. DAMARIG
_____

18. SMCIMEAGR
_____

19. ISYON
_____

20. HTTWRA
_____

Football Puzzle 16

1. ERTNTAHE   _____

2. HSKAAWSE   _____

3. LALC   _____

4. MAEMTTAE   _____

5. AGREAVE   _____

6. CCHAO   _____

7. INCLIDPEIS   _____

8. AEFM   _____

9. SOLS   _____

10. DINW   _____

11. SYOFALFP   _____

12. RWTOH   _____

13. GENERE   _____

14. NCGIOSR   _____

15. TAOTIRSP   _____

16. IEEFSVFNO   _____

17. CFESHI   _____

18. WLSIE   _____

19. GISALN   _____

20. FESNITS   _____

SOLUTIONS

1. GORHU   ROUGH

2. EEVRWS   SWERVE

3. NOPMHCAI   CHAMPION

4. ISNWG   SWING

5. EAMYHM   MAYHEM

6. DINVIISO   DIVISION

7. GDUZEORRI   RODRIGUEZ

8. EBRRA   BERRA

9. EREJ   JEER

10. ALGUEE   LEAGUE

11. ETASS   ASSET

12. STYMES   SYSTEM

13. ITEOCYLV   VELOCITY

14. ERA   ERA

15. ERTHTA   THREAT

16. FOIVFSNEE   OFFENSIVE

17. OPTPIOTNYRU   OPPORTUNITY

18. EEFTGIRYCLIN   ELECTRIFYING

19. LEVOG   GLOVE

20. TIOTOMNPCEI   COMPETITION

Baseball Puzzle 1

1. KURQI   QUIRK

2. PRTESVEPIEC   PERSPECTIVE

3. UAGRONDES   DANGEROUS

4. UIDIATNO   AUDITION

5. TNSRAIPAOLNII INSPIRATIONAL

6. HRIEGG   GEHRIG

7. PEIOSDDL   LOPSIDED

8. ZNFREY   FRENZY

9. UTCLANUP   PUNCTUAL

10. DRUEOTLFEI   OUTFIELDER

11. BSLABLAE   BASEBALL

12. TRCOREC   CORRECT

13. WROTH   THROW

14. OUNMATIOCMNIC COMMUNICATION

15. LBIEIEGL   ELIGIBLE

16. ERFELI   RELIEF

17. BPNELUL   BULLPEN

18. RRHOYWUSTTT   TRUSTWORTHY

19. RPOTNOTCEI   PROTECTION

20. CMSMAERIG   SCRIMMAGE

Baseball Puzzle 2

1. BRONSINO	ROBINSON
2. SOSA	SOSA
3. GDTUUO	DUGOUT
4. CEHRTCA	CATCHER
5. OTRIYVC	VICTORY
6. CBOB	COBB
7. TEAETOING	NEGOTIATE
8. TOWAMRKE	TEAMWORK
9. ILSNE	LINES
10. NCIOITONDNIG	CONDITIONING
11. HRTDI	THIRD
12. UNRNER	RUNNER
13. CTTLSEAIH	ATHLETICS
14. BKRCI	BRICK
15. ISPTERA	PIRATES
16. NCOURNAEN	ANNOUNCER
17. TCIPH	PITCH
18. BJATIOLIUN	JUBILATION
19. DODINKASABCM	DIAMONDBACKS
20. TSMRSNPOPE	PROMPTNESS

Baseball Puzzle 3

61

#	Scrambled	Answer
1.	NSAITG	GIANTS
2.	TALEP	PLATE
3.	RIB	RBI
4.	DTAEPU	UPDATE
5.	TCCHEAARR	CHARACTER
6.	DABEORCSOR	SCOREBOARD
7.	TEARBT	BATTER
8.	NTTOYROEI	NOTORIETY
9.	FGYEFRI	GRIFFEY
10.	LINNPGNA	PLANNING
11.	ETTHELA	ATHLETE
12.	EOSLESSCR	SCORELESS
13.	CRSHU	CRUSH
14.	TIPLLABS	SPITBALL
15.	CLCETAEPS	SPECTACLE
16.	FULO	FOUL
17.	CKQIU	QUICK
18.	STHFI	SHIFT
19.	HACCO	COACH
20.	ALED	LEAD

Baseball Puzzle 4

1. LUOSEUCHB   CLUBHOUSE

2. RTESSS   STRESS

3. MTCMOMIENT   COMMITMENT

4. ATIASMN   STAMINA

5. LUATBR   BRUTAL

6. DEISLNDIB   BLINDSIDE

7. PLITS-SOENDC   SPLIT-SECOND

8. CISITTASST   STATISTICS

9. IRCGSON   SCORING

10. IUESRTVCNTI   INSTRUCTIVE

11. HEUSLEDC   SCHEDULE

12. IGNLSE   SINGLE

13. UARFCTER   FRACTURE

14. IGIRTANN   TRAINING

15. GUNEYRC   URGENCY

16. ANEEVRBLUL   VULNERABLE

17. ELSLY   YELLS

18. EONTCTS   CONTEST

19. SUDTPEI   DISPUTE

20. OINOTVA   OVATION

Baseball Puzzle 5

1.	GEAM	GAME
2.	OSNMRUFI	UNIFORMS
3.	LKISL	SKILL
4.	LITRAEETELINCOG	INTERCOLLEGIATE
5.	SEULMSC	MUSCLES
6.	OTHIITSLY	HOSTILITY
7.	YEIRAVT	VARIETY
8.	DEDEEBALPN	DEPENDABLE
9.	ENTEREEFCNRI	INTERFERENCE
10.	GAER	GEAR
11.	HSRTLSEU	RUTHLESS
12.	FTBAALLS	FASTBALL
13.	NNNBGEURAIS	BASERUNNING
14.	GLEIMEATTI	LEGITIMATE
15.	ORHNIGLEL	HOLLERING
16.	EEHRBLCSA	BLEACHERS
17.	TTAAINLOIER	RETALIATION
18.	ITUETATD	ATTITUDE
19.	PDRASE	PADRES
20.	STAANDSDR	STANDARDS

Baseball Puzzle 6

1.	OHWORRTVEN	OVERTHROWN
2.	ICSKERO	ROCKIES
3.	TIHS	HITS
4.	OSLS	LOSS
5.	KDEC	DECK
6.	ETI	TIE
7.	RUICETR	RECRUIT
8.	EISSOBONS	OBSESSION
9.	RYAS	RAYS
10.	EMEWASO	AWESOME
11.	EIRNIFLED	INFIELDER
12.	CRSAIHAM	CHARISMA
13.	IALVIGNT	VIGILANT
14.	YRALL	RALLY
15.	IETCTVADA	ACTIVATED
16.	NEETMQUIP	EQUIPMENT
17.	NBRHOAITLIAITE	REHABILITATION
18.	LDEIS	SLIDE
19.	ERNCEXEIEP	EXPERIENCE
20.	RLCKSOE	LOCKERS

Baseball Puzzle 7

1. FYOFLSAP — PLAYOFFS

2. IBALITY — ABILITY

3. DMUNO — MOUND

4. EMTESE — ESTEEM

5. LSEEIINDS — SIDELINES

6. ITVNEETAT — ATTENTIVE

7. YTIULQA — QUALITY

8. REECNT — CENTER

9. RWSDAA — AWARDS

10. EITAMOVT — MOTIVATE

11. RPEISAHELD — LEADERSHIP

12. AEAR — AREA

13. MLBFUE — FUMBLE

14. SDTSAN — STANDS

15. HABARLDL — HARDBALL

16. NIW — WIN

17. IOSNY — NOISY

18. VTICTIAY — ACTIVITY

19. GEMSA — GAMES

20. CNEMGUETENORA — ENCOURAGEMENT

Baseball Puzzle 8

1.	TIRANTOO	ROTATION
2.	AODDINM	DIAMOND
3.	BAVEULCRL	CURVEBALL
4.	SCISCAL	CLASSIC
5.	ULBC	CLUB
6.	RPTLIE	TRIPLE
7.	ZNOE	ZONE
8.	SANUULU	UNUSUAL
9.	SHECIT	ETHICS
10.	APESRI	PRAISE
11.	RIESED	DESIRE
12.	ONSEDC	SECOND
13.	RKUWOTO	WORKOUT
14.	SIGTARN	RATINGS
15.	FENSEDE	DEFENSE
16.	ANF-FTES	FAN-FEST
17.	NOEWR	OWNER
18.	ERI	IRE
19.	IWSTN	TWINS
20.	SENMSEI	NEMESIS

Baseball Puzzle 9

1. PILIAMRTA   IMPARTIAL

2. OPNTIEENRV   PREVENTION

3. BOPERITDIH   PROHIBITED

4. UTO   OUT

5. EERRSBW   BREWERS

6. TBA   BAT

7. ATMEATEM   TEAMMATE

8. NSEMETEMARU   MEASUREMENT

9. ITMT   MITT

10. ROCSE   SCORE

11. REPTFEC   PERFECT

12. YNASKEE   YANKEES

13. NMEAEC   MENACE

14. TIZINOAAORNG   ORGANIZATION

15. AOMEITND   DOMINATE

16. GIIWNNN   WINNING

17. NAOAR   AARON

18. ESAB   BASE

19. RLBANEEOSA   REASONABLE

20. AMNABSE   BASEMAN

Baseball Puzzle 10

1. NEKE   KEEN

2. TDARF   DRAFT

3. RINKPE   RIPKEN

4. RNLSDCAIA   CARDINALS

5. CPAEGTEREN   PERCENTAGE

6. OAREEPRNMCF   PERFORMANCE

7. PNELAS   PLANES

8. ECEHR   CHEER

9. OTOANCNNIFTOR   CONFRONTATION

10. OESUTRPNISTI   SUPERSTITION

11. UBCLNKKELAL   KNUCKLEBALL

12. SEOL   LOSE

13. RONGEI   REGION

14. EPEDS   SPEED

15. BNLERCTAIEO   CELEBRATION

16. TNAETL   TALENT

17. PCRAEAPNEA   APPEARANCE

18. IDCMAYN   DYNAMIC

19. ONRITVAIA   VARIATION

20. YYLATLO   LOYALTY

Baseball Puzzle 11

1. THACC   CATCH

2. TUCEEXE   EXECUTE

3. LLA-RATS   ALL-STAR

4. EOLFUCRF   FORCEFUL

5. IRGCENTEE   ENERGETIC

6. IPMASET   PASTIME

7. YTTUNIAQ   QUANTITY

8. ETKICST   TICKETS

9. WATRTH   THWART

10. ITFTREOUD   FORTITUDE

11. VUATL   VAULT

12. IFCIFLAO   OFFICIAL

13. ACOLL   LOCAL

14. ERCTIHP   PITCHER

15. AEZL   ZEAL

16. TFSIR   FIRST

17. ELXRMPEYA   EXEMPLARY

18. OSGRDED   DODGERS

19. AAUCCYRC   ACCURACY

20. ITSCIE   CITIES

Baseball Puzzle 12

1. DEUGICAN   GUIDANCE

2. SRAEGAEV   AVERAGES

3. ILSRIETEN   RESILIENT

4. ATICAPORPEIN APPRECIATION

5. EIOUNTACS   TENACIOUS

6. COFDNENECI   CONFIDENCE

7. NNPPEOOT   OPPONENT

8. ESTPECENRIS   PERSISTENCE

9. SRATTS   STARTS

10. PRAYLSE   PLAYERS

11. OECFR   FORCE

12. UTISCGON   SCOUTING

13. ISOOIPTN   POSITION

14. SORTP   SPORT

15. AURSSITOSD   DISASTROUS

16. FSLTOALB   SOFTBALL

17. PTANLYE   PENALTY

18. JYO   JOY

19. ZAIGZG   ZIGZAG

20. OPEHAIUR   EUPHORIA

Baseball Puzzle 13

1. NWEDID   WINDED

2. DOMICIATEN   MEDICATION

3. ESGESVRAGI   AGGRESSIVE

4. FLTE-AHEDNR   LEFT-HANDER

5. PPSNSSTROMHAI   SPORTSMANSHIP

6. TEAEFD   DEFEAT

7. OTRT   TROT

8. LCAL   CALL

9. BINHAS   BANISH

10. BKLA   BALK

11. OSLJUP   PUJOLS

12. ELSOUZA   ZEALOUS

13. OSSRSPON   SPONSORS

14. MAESCNICH   MECHANICS

15. ROUECGAUOS   COURAGEOUS

16. TAMCOEILB   METABOLIC

17. KLWA   WALK

18. IESHLPIL   PHILLIES

19. ROUT   TOUR

20. PITCAM   IMPACT

Baseball Puzzle 14

#	Scrambled	Unscrambled
1.	LRONTOC	CONTROL
2.	RINOETPAOCO	COOPERATION
3.	AOGL	GOAL
4.	USBC	CUBS
5.	SISTENNTOC	CONSISTENT
6.	SISEER	SERIES
7.	INEIIGBELL	INELIGIBLE
8.	FERILED	FIELDER
9.	ESRD	REDS
10.	ETJRE	JETER
11.	KNRIAGN	RANKING
12.	EDIORITNC	DIRECTION
13.	TMEA	TEAM
14.	NNIGATUD	DAUNTING
15.	TMACMOREMEO	COMMEMORATE
16.	TLHMEE	HELMET
17.	NETLTORA	TOLERANT
18.	FEAS	SAFE
19.	GAT	TAG
20.	UMIPCNGO	UPCOMING

Baseball Puzzle 15

1.	HOEM	HOME
2.	RNASMIER	MARINERS
3.	OTHRPTSSO	SHORTSTOP
4.	MTOPISMI	OPTIMISM
5.	OFSEENF	OFFENSE
6.	ECUNADREN	ENDURANCE
7.	NIINNG	INNING
8.	ALBL	BALL
9.	NBACLAE	BALANCE
10.	TRNEI-LGEAUE	INTER-LEAGUE
11.	MNSTEAUISH	ENTHUSIASM
12.	EPPTAROIARN	PREPARATION
13.	PMV	MVP
14.	NRSOTTICUOB	OBSTRUCTION
15.	X-YASR	X-RAYS
16.	APAPEL	APPEAL
17.	XIAMEMZI	MAXIMIZE
18.	NROFCCEEEN	CONFERENCE
19.	SUSITURNODI	INDUSTRIOUS
20.	YARLL-THA	RALLY-HAT

Baseball Puzzle 16

1. AFNS   FANS

2. EVUOSRGI   GRIEVOUS

3. ICPSMNPAIOHH   CHAMPIONSHIP

4. ORSTSA   ASTROS

5. ABLLERIE   RELIABLE

6. ORSE   ROSE

7. ESNPSSOOSI   POSSESSION

8. AELTS   STEAL

9. SOSEAN   SEASON

10. TNDUIE   UNITED

11. MLBNEI   NIMBLE

12. FIDLIEN   INFIELD

13. ULSRGGE   SLUGGER

14. TOLNSE   STOLEN

15. NEATBE   BEATEN

16. PRNIST   SPRINT

17. RVPNESEREECA   PERSEVERANCE

18. UMIORNF   UNIFORM

19. ESMT   METS

20. ERTOCPWONSO   COOPERSTOWN

Baseball Puzzle 17

75

1.	SVSEA	SAVES
2.	ORUPLPA	POPULAR
3.	NUISSTICTNRO	INSTRUCTIONS
4.	KRSETI	STRIKE
5.	ERKJ	JERK
6.	DILEF	FIELD
7.	DRAC	CARD
8.	IBNONDG	BONDING
9.	ONRERSLCAVTOI	CONTROVERSIAL
10.	ADGEVANAT	ADVANTAGE
11.	EBULOD	DOUBLE
12.	ADACTSBOR	BROADCAST
13.	ICSDNIIPEL	DISCIPLINE
14.	FTIOLEUD	OUTFIELD
15.	ELIVREOSD	OVERSLIDE
16.	FOSOISALRNPE	PROFESSIONAL
17.	DERAWR	REWARD
18.	TBBOYA	BATBOY
19.	PRKA	PARK
20.	TRWHYO	WORTHY

Baseball Puzzle 18

1. KIRMIHSS   SKIRMISH

2. SILGNA   SIGNAL

3. SINETEN   INTENSE

4. STEGRI   TIGERS

5. NBDOS   BONDS

6. EOHRM   HOMER

7. JDUEG   JUDGE

8. TUBN   BUNT

9. MEAAGNR   MANAGER

10. RBSAVE   BRAVES

11. ELITGNID   DILIGENT

12. MLTEAN   MANTLE

13. SKAETR   STREAK

14. CWORSD   CROWDS

15. AUIDTSM   STADIUM

16. YHOTRP   TROPHY

17. RSNETGTH   STRENGTH

18. RIEARTN   TRAINER

19. EEWPS   SWEEP

20. PRCAITCE   PRACTICE

Baseball Puzzle 19

1.	EGALLIL	ILLEGAL
2.	SQDUA	SQUAD
3.	NO-ERTHIT	NO-HITTER
4.	YRAPEL	PLAYER
5.	LAROSY	ROYALS
6.	OMCMNO-ENSSE	COMMON-SENSE
7.	GARNRES	RANGERS
8.	FARI	FAIR
9.	EAULIFR	FAILURE
10.	BVREIOAH	BEHAVIOR
11.	VECIFFTEE	EFFECTIVE
12.	ISTSAS	ASSIST
13.	CTPRIIAOANPTI	PARTICIPATION
14.	OSELRIO	ORIOLES
15.	EGTASYRT	STRATEGY
16.	REECRA	CAREER
17.	LAVELUBA	VALUABLE
18.	UAGHLETR	LAUGHTER
19.	AONVSBERT	OBSERVANT
20.	DNIUNOB	INBOUND

Baseball Puzzle 20

1. OTIAUNNGTDS   OUTSTANDING

2. HISNIPK   KINSHIP

3. NRTANSGDAD   GRANDSTAND

4. EMRUIP   UMPIRE

5. AYDR   YARD

6. GRNIOCOEITN   RECOGNITION

7. NTVEROMIMEP   IMPROVEMENT

8. NNIADSI   INDIANS

9. TFROEIF   FORFEIT

10. AVLTRE   TRAVEL

11. INNE   NINE

12. EESSURPR   PRESSURE

13. SEJINRIU   INJURIES

14. SAMY   MAYS

15. GOYNU   YOUNG

16. THRU   RUTH

17. KZIUUS   SUZUKI

18. RNU   RUN

19. UIELNP   LINEUP

20. TNLOIANAS   NATIONALS

Baseball Puzzle 21

79

1. SDENLESII   SIDELINES

2. SCIITSSTTA   STATISTICS

3. TFI   FIT

4. OTP   OPT

5. OTHS   SHOT

6. THCCUL   CLUTCH

7. CREHSTT   STRETCH

8. PMEECRFRONA   PERFORMANCE

9. NAF   FAN

10. IMIITANAONG   IMAGINATION

11. OTPSSASOEN   POSTSEASON

12. TPACEIRC   PRACTICE

13. LGAO   GOAL

14. OSRCE   SCORE

15. OPMSITMI   OPTIMISM

16. CCIRTLIA   CRITICAL

17. JSNOONH   JOHNSON

18. SNOIPITO   POSITION

19. USSN   SUNS

20. XMAMIZIE   MAXIMIZE

Basketball Puzzle 1

1. RLUEARG   REGULAR

2. PERACS   PACERS

3. IMTGIN   TIMING

4. TLAHEH   HEALTH

5. BRDI   BIRD

6. OGTIORNNCIE   RECOGNITION

7. ITRIPS   SPIRIT

8. SMSELUC   MUSCLES

9. IDULNVDIIA   INDIVIDUAL

10. RCIEPE   PIERCE

11. IUYQALT   QUALITY

12. RANTDU   DURANT

13. EDBUORN   REBOUND

14. SAPLCOEL   COLLAPSE

15. NIBELESS   SENSIBLE

16. RTORER   TERROR

17. FTVAIREO   FAVORITE

18. YRUCR   CURRY

19. AMGIC   MAGIC

20. YHRYHEIOAPTSP   PHYSIOTHERAPY

Basketball Puzzle 2

1. SEAV   SAVE

2. MLUABR   LUMBAR

3. CLHSSRHIPAO   SCHOLARSHIP

4. SDRCTTNEIEUR   UNRESTRICTED

5. NDORMA   RODMAN

6. ICSAARHM   CHARISMA

7. BTRYNA   BRYANT

8. AYDCMNI   DYNAMIC

9. OCITAANTTR   ATTRACTION

10. IATLR   TRAIL

11. NRYTIASA   SANITARY

12. MEBUFL   FUMBLE

13. NGETSUG   NUGGETS

14. RHSU   RUSH

15. NTOISP   POINTS

16. RRITAY   RARITY

17. YHAOOR   HOORAY

18. EOMSTRR   TREMORS

19. MRNANTUOTE   TOURNAMENT

20. RTSEID   STRIDE

Basketball Puzzle 3

1.	EASCR	SCARE
2.	SIVOEPTI	POSITIVE
3.	SLILK	SKILL
4.	LOLIODWG	GOODWILL
5.	AINRTRE	TRAINER
6.	ESTRNEIRTVAEPE	REPRESENTATIVE
7.	RTINGIAN	TRAINING
8.	SNIRGOC	SCORING
9.	CROORSDBAE	SCOREBOARD
10.	SLLUB	BULLS
11.	EUNTRVRO	TURNOVER
12.	NORITNEEVP	PREVENTION
13.	TTTMEPA	ATTEMPT
14.	RTOT	TROT
15.	TIEM	TIME
16.	ANLEL	ALLEN
17.	IEURSTMO	MOISTURE
18.	PUTITAHEERC	THERAPEUTIC
19.	GFRTNALA	FLAGRANT
20.	SOTEV	VOTES

Basketball Puzzle 4

1. UMEARSE   MEASURE

2. SNPUISNESO   SUSPENSION

3. ETIFIDC   DEFICIT

4. NEWIC   WINCE

5. AILUCRC   CRUCIAL

6. NEFEITB   BENEFIT

7. ERLYPA   PLAYER

8. NIDLIIVOAS   DIVISIONAL

9. TROIYCV   VICTORY

10. DONAJR   JORDAN

11. ONITUNCF   FUNCTION

12. IAFFCOTEI   OFFICIATE

13. TEISLCC   CELTICS

14. EURLLSS   RUSSELL

15. DEGLEN   LEGEND

16. NSITTPSRUEOI   SUPERSTITION

17. ORDWHA   HOWARD

18. ESAACSTSNI   ASSISTANCE

19. REIGVN   ERVING

20. AESTKR   STREAK

Basketball Puzzle 5

1. NGSIK   KINGS

2. EVARCLSAI   CAVALIERS

3. GETVAANAD   ADVANTAGE

4. RRAGPOM   PROGRAM

5. EODIRP   PERIOD

6. TEBHR   BERTH

7. OTNTIXLAEA   EXALTATION

8. IENIYTNST   INTENSITY

9. LGNOIS   LOSING

10. IRQVUE   QUIVER

11. SURDG   DRUGS

12. BTROVINIA   VIBRATION

13. IAWSZDR   WIZARDS

14. ASTNCACOIU   ACCUSATION

15. ZAJZ   JAZZ

16. MAGSMUINY   GYMNASIUM

17. WHEIG   WEIGH

18. BYAREKL   BARKLEY

19. DGRAU   GUARD

20. STWE   WEST

Basketball Puzzle 6

85

1. NOABIIAIHRETTL   REHABILITATION

2. ISNSMEE   NEMESIS

3. ECSOKTR   ROCKETS

4. HNLCCI   CLINCH

5. AGREEECNTP   PERCENTAGE

6. UHOTY   YOUTH

7. NOIMRPGIS   PROMISING

8. QCIUK   QUICK

9. TINODINOIGNC   CONDITIONING

10. ROTOS   TORSO

11. ZTLKU   KLUTZ

12. PWEOR   POWER

13. GYNEICHI   HYGIENIC

14. CLNEHITAC   TECHNICAL

15. ATLIVOOIN   VIOLATION

16. URNYIJ   INJURY

17. RBILDEB   DRIBBLE

18. TINAOTIVOM   MOTIVATION

19. TROEBSLWMIVE   TIMBERWOLVES

20. NIICMOPETTO   COMPETITION

Basketball Puzzle 7

1. LEOMATIIINN   ELIMINATION

2. HRECAIMLNAB   CHAMBERLAIN

3. SSERUERP   PRESSURE

4. ESIINLTRE   RESILIENT

5. POMIAHCN   CHAMPION

6. UHRDTNE   THUNDER

7. NIISDOIV   DIVISION

8. ETAYRSTG   STRATEGY

9. LSOO   SOLO

10. IFCNEOITN   INFECTION

11. VCTOUORSII   VICTORIOUS

12. EIHNEYG   HYGIENE

13. MEMOYR   MEMORY

14. EKRNIDD   KINDRED

15. AFEETD   DEFEAT

16. SMPYMSTO   SYMPTOMS

17. SDEEENF   DEFENSE

18. SGMAE   GAMES

19. KCIP   PICK

20. HOPO   HOOP

Basketball Puzzle 8

1. EDRLEA   LEADER

2. UCOIETESCNV   CONSECUTIVE

3. OSNESA   SEASON

4. YITLTIBAS   STABILITY

5. TSRAERT   STARTER

6. EDRIV   DRIVE

7. ZEIS   SIZE

8. DAINGSNT   STANDING

9. OTTNPE   POTENT

10. KBSATE   BASKET

11. ORESNOPSIFAL   PROFESSIONAL

12. ADWE   WADE

13. ALNESCIP   PELICANS

14. KRNA   RANK

15. NAAC   NCAA

16. NRGAMI   MARGIN

17. EMOTACLIB   METABOLIC

18. LSERPCPI   CLIPPERS

19. PRGI   GRIP

20. VESRREE   RESERVE

Basketball Puzzle 9

1. ANRSORETIPIP   PERSPIRATION

2. XEIESCRE   EXERCISE

3. ASCOASNTITFI   SATISFACTION

4. OMREIEVT   OVERTIME

5. LWOJNUAO   OLAJUWON

6. MSJEA   JAMES

7. INWNING   WINNING

8. SVLDCAAIRUROCA   CARDIOVASCULAR

9. EZRLSAB   BLAZERS

10. WNI   WIN

11. TGTRNSHE   STRENGTH

12. ANDIEEDL   DEADLINE

13. ESDASIE   DISEASE

14. ELAKATLBBS   BASKETBALL

15. OLSS   LOSS

16. MMEEATTA   TEAMMATE

17. AITPESENL   PENALTIES

18. IDLDPESO   LOPSIDED

19. SEBT   BEST

20. ABLL   BALL

Basketball Puzzle 10

1. ELRZZGISI	GRIZZLIES
2. LNIIASFT	FINALIST
3. CDORER	RECORD
4. LROE	ROLE
5. RENCTITOPO	PROTECTION
6. OSNESSER	SORENESS
7. ENGYRE	ENERGY
8. JMUP	JUMP
9. TAIVNAL	VALIANT
10. IRDBNBLIG	DRIBBLING
11. TENEANTADC	ATTENDANCE
12. RIRAWSRO	WARRIORS
13. OCWRD	CROWD
14. BEUNCO	BOUNCE
15. ESZT	ZEST
16. ONCRETRIITS	RESTRICTION
17. CIDIRSNOTAT	DISTRACTION
18. ENDDEF	DEFEND
19. TNOPISS	PISTONS
20. LCPIUB	PUBLIC

Basketball Puzzle 11

1. SMITNSSAPOHPR   SPORTSMANSHIP

2. LSOE   SOLE

3. NEAALCB   BALANCE

4. RPCETTO   PROTECT

5. ZROE   ZERO

6. RONTIEU   ROUTINE

7. ANNOHYT   ANTHONY

8. IRPEWROEF   FIREPOWER

9. UEELGA   LEAGUE

10. UDNCNA   DUNCAN

11. LUYCK   LUCKY

12. SLUAUUN   UNUSUAL

13. DASQU   QUADS

14. OTNTPROPYUI   OPPORTUNITY

15. UBTEOAKR   OUTBREAK

16. PIENPP   PIPPEN

17. AONTIANL   NATIONAL

18. NAEROTLIGU   REGULATION

19. TANDVEIILA   INVALIDATE

20. MIEOTNXEP   EXEMPTION

Basketball Puzzle 12

1.	VEAIW	WAIVE
2.	ISMTANHI	NAISMITH
3.	ZREUBZ	BUZZER
4.	IPMIPCAOHNSH	CHAMPIONSHIP
5.	NAHS	NASH
6.	ZASPIMEEH	EMPHASIZE
7.	ASKLRE	LAKERS
8.	USBCK	BUCKS
9.	IEQUNU	UNIQUE
10.	ATIEMDCINO	MEDICATION
11.	YEK	KEY
12.	SENOB	BONES
13.	REOFC	FORCE
14.	NROIOMT	MONITOR
15.	MTTIUOE	TIMEOUT
16.	TICNTORAIAPIP	PARTICIPATION
17.	ALTYIBI	ABILITY
18.	LEZA	ZEAL
19.	LTHEYAH	HEALTHY
20.	CNAOUNENNMET	ANNOUNCEMENT

Basketball Puzzle 13

1.	TSTE	TEST
2.	GEILYNL	YELLING
3.	CMESHE	SCHEME
4.	HEERBTA	BREATHE
5.	VSAAEEGR	AVERAGES
6.	LXFE	FLEX
7.	VCAMRESI	MAVERICS
8.	MNROYLCA	NORMALCY
9.	KISD	SKID
10.	RMAENAG	MANAGER
11.	ITKINOZW	NOWITZKI
12.	NOCRCFNEEE	CONFERENCE
13.	OOCNTTKS	STOCKTON
14.	TONE	TONE
15.	TWUKOOR	WORKOUT
16.	NSTAAMI	STAMINA
17.	RCEUTRI	RECRUIT
18.	ROEUGCA	COURAGE
19.	AEMASGS	MASSAGE
20.	PNIEOSSSOS	POSSESSION

Basketball Puzzle 14

93

1. MEAT   TEAM

2. OTHS   HOST

3. ADNREH   HARDEN

4. NEERTC   CENTER

5. SNEAIPSATO   PASSIONATE

6. IPNAC   PANIC

7. SRYTU   RUSTY

8. RYEREOCV   RECOVERY

9. TEHSNRO   HORNETS

10. YDBO   BODY

11. ERORSR   ERRORS

12. OTOCDR   DOCTOR

13. RKSI   RISK

14. DOSIWM   WISDOM

15. SRPUS   SPURS

16. MISS   MISS

17. ORADABKBC   BACKBOARD

18. OMAELN   MALONE

19. TTIAOVEM   MOTIVATE

20. LISOATECUPN   SPECULATION

Basketball Puzzle 15

1. TNPIOO OPTION

2. INWGE EWING

3. ETROONRBS ROBERTSON

4. IEACVT ACTIVE

5. HCCAO COACH

6. STIITICENVN INSTINCTIVE

7. NSARIT STRAIN

8. EIT TIE

9. WHIEGTS WEIGHTS

10. NEEFSOVIF OFFENSIVE

11. ATVAPEITC CAPTIVATE

12. HOOSP HOOPS

13. EEKP KEEP

14. VLAOR VALOR

15. DSTGINTANUO OUTSTANDING

16. LTHTAEE ATHLETE

17. LERAETANT ALTERNATE

18. DREECNNUA ENDURANCE

19. UNDK DUNK

20. RTUH HURT

Basketball Puzzle 16

95

1.	TFAUWHCL	WATCHFUL
2.	TETLAB	BATTLE
3.	MEKFOWRRA	FRAMEWORK
4.	AVIESRGSEG	AGGRESSIVE
5.	ALIHTTCSE	ATHLETICS
6.	ORUTC	COURT
7.	WIRST	WRIST
8.	NTSE	NETS
9.	OTSGNR	STRONG
10.	TRPUPOS	SUPPORT
11.	OCLIFAIF	OFFICIAL
12.	LEPYRXMEA	EXEMPLARY
13.	ZIIMMEIN	MINIMIZE
14.	ECIXTIGN	EXCITING
15.	FLOU	FOUL
16.	AXRLE	RELAX
17.	OTONDINCAOIR	COORDINATION
18.	EHTA	HEAT
19.	ETBRHA	BREATH
20.	MEGA	GAME

Basketball Puzzle 17

1.	LOGRAEIN	REGIONAL
2.	SIKNCK	KNICKS
3.	SSISTA	ASSIST
4.	EOSL	LOSE
5.	PORASRT	RAPTORS
6.	WAHSK	HAWKS
7.	TASNEISREC	RESISTANCE
8.	ERPNIERNTTTIAO	INTERPRETATION
9.	RPLEEAC	REPLACE
10.	TPINROTCEEIN	INTERCEPTION
11.	GJNARO	JARGON
12.	PAEYHRT	THERAPY
13.	VBABILEUELNE	UNBELIEVABLE
14.	UMLPS	SLUMP
15.	PAURCMYSE	SUPREMACY
16.	GCONINCIVN	CONVINCING
17.	PYFETRI	PETRIFY
18.	DIET	DIET
19.	WRKO	WORK
20.	ISHATGRMN	HAMSTRING

Basketball Puzzle 18

1. SORSBCAR	CROSSBAR
2. EALOZUS	ZEALOUS
3. ASEBR	BEARS
4. LAGO	GOAL
5. ATPRETN	PATTERN
6. PCIK	PICK
7. AROLYT	TAYLOR
8. TEANBE	BEATEN
9. EMFBUL	FUMBLE
10. MYEMAH	MAYHEM
11. YTICEOVL	VELOCITY
12. OBOSNRC	BRONCOS
13. LEBGNAS	BENGALS
14. CALSFNO	FALCONS
15. RUNEMBS	NUMBERS
16. FAL	AFL
17. FDEATE	DEFEAT
18. UCCEBANSRE	BUCCANEERS
19. NITRSA	STRAIN
20. UCHRS	CRUSH

Football Puzzle 1

1. NITOOZNIARAG ORGANIZATION

2. IMMA MAIM

3. POTOSH PHOTOS

4. MRIECSMAOLC COMMERCIALS

5. CECESPLTA SPECTACLE

6. STHIIOLTY HOSTILITY

7. TSCEAHC CATCHES

8. COFRE FORCE

9. IMEFIDLD MIDFIELD

10. ASNP SNAP

11. JOGANR JARGON

12. RSRGHECA CHARGERS

13. WTEHI WHITE

14. GNRDOAUES DANGEROUS

15. IMCITEOTOPN COMPETITION

16. YJO JOY

17. AEGMS GAMES

18. TOTIMEU TIMEOUT

19. NLLIEEIIGB INELIGIBLE

20. EPDHIRSAEL LEADERSHIP

Football Puzzle 2

1.	X-YRAS	X-RAYS
2.	LFAH	HALF
3.	NTOIDUNSGTA	OUTSTANDING
4.	TRAIAETIONL	RETALIATION
5.	IHST	HITS
6.	EUTEECX	EXECUTE
7.	IOTOPPRUNYT	OPPORTUNITY
8.	TEYHLHA	HEALTHY
9.	UUSTBK	BUTKUS
10.	SOOTB	BOOST
11.	ENIRHSEN	ENSHRINE
12.	RRDOIING	GRIDIRON
13.	IPOSSSNEOS	POSSESSION
14.	LAZE	ZEAL
15.	RKACTABQEUR	QUARTERBACK
16.	HPTGAASUOR	AUTOGRAPHS
17.	QREUVI	QUIVER
18.	EERCSH	CHEERS
19.	DSITORSE	STEROIDS
20.	EILTESNIR	RESILIENT

Football Puzzle 3

1.	NLTVEIO	VIOLENT
2.	MSRA	RAMS
3.	IHTSM	SMITH
4.	NDIIISOV	DIVISION
5.	OIDSPNLH	DOLPHINS
6.	NIEPELMCOT	INCOMPLETE
7.	CIRVPTSEEEP	PERSPECTIVE
8.	CECSSSU	SUCCESS
9.	MASACHRI	CHARISMA
10.	SNAREDS	SANDERS
11.	EPSWE	SWEEP
12.	TIAYVRE	VARIETY
13.	GTLIAELCOE	COLLEGIATE
14.	BUNIDON	INBOUND
15.	ECTNORGIONI	RECOGNITION
16.	ISNPAOS	PASSION
17.	PSRTO	SPORT
18.	EYRGADA	YARDAGE
19.	GNVIIKS	VIKINGS
20.	ILLKS	SKILL

Football Puzzle 4

101

1.	ONAITVARI	VARIATION
2.	SCRDBAOAT	BROADCAST
3.	GTROETHE	TOGETHER
4.	GIWN	WING
5.	AEYTPNL	PENALTY
6.	OHEICDW	COWHIDE
7.	SCLKOER	LOCKERS
8.	TBINAREOHATIIL	REHABILITATION
9.	SEROC	SCORE
10.	ROGHU	ROUGH
11.	CCYCAAUR	ACCURACY
12.	SWBNOR	BROWNS
13.	TIUCRRE	RECRUIT
14.	JKRE	JERK
15.	EAAGNRM	MANAGER
16.	IRE	IRE
17.	DRNALOTTAII	TRADITIONAL
18.	IBAITYL	ABILITY
19.	RECI	RICE
20.	SLCOT	COLTS

Football Puzzle 5

1. EEAGUL   LEAGUE

2. RATEFRUC   FRACTURE

3. OCENISID   DECISION

4. LYIQAUF   QUALIFY

5. LLEYS   YELLS

6. CORTIYV   VICTORY

7. SHIRISKM   SKIRMISH

8. KIDLCEAFB   BACKFIELD

9. ERECCFEONN   CONFERENCE

10. IET   TIE

11. TEAM   TEAM

12. DEN-NEZO   END-ZONE

13. ACJNOSK   JACKSON

14. NAGNNIM   MANNING

15. TOIANPCTIRIPA   PARTICIPATION

16. ENTETIOAG   NEGOTIATE

17. TGTESHNR   STRENGTH

18. TTOL   LOTT

19. UFFECROL   FORCEFUL

20. SESRTS   STRESS

Football Puzzle 6

1. NNRACNUOE   ANNOUNCER

2. BECAANL   BALANCE

3. TARRQEU   QUARTER

4. ERALYSP   PLAYERS

5. RJEE   JEER

6. EEHTLTA   ATHLETE

7. ELEXC   EXCEL

8. EVRESRE   RESERVE

9. BFUALLKC   FULLBACK

10. AEDDTNICIO   DEDICATION

11. HSVAEL   HALVES

12. RIECDNITO   DIRECTION

13. RITNIONETEPC   INTERCEPTION

14. WGERAGS   SWAGGER

15. REOBACCRKN   CORNERBACK

16. RNEVOTRU   TURNOVER

17. TMVTIOAE   MOTIVATE

18. FATDR   DRAFT

19. ATRULB   BRUTAL

20. TRPISI   SPIRIT

Football Puzzle 7

1.	SLSTEERE	STEELERS
2.	RKETAS	STREAK
3.	ISNUIJER	INJURIES
4.	RAVLI	RIVAL
5.	NRCUGEY	URGENCY
6.	EIPNSANXO	EXPANSION
7.	UQICK	QUICK
8.	LTEKCA	TACKLE
9.	NSRTADDAS	STANDARDS
10.	LPRATOPYIU	POPULARITY
11.	SRITODAUSS	DISASTROUS
12.	OGNOCTNIDINI	CONDITIONING
13.	LAEDRE	LEADER
14.	AAILDNRSC	CARDINALS
15.	EYNZRF	FRENZY
16.	UNRAEECND	ENDURANCE
17.	PLLAEARL	PARALLEL
18.	NEMLBI	NIMBLE
19.	NOCATUI	CAUTION
20.	ITLET	TITLE

Football Puzzle 8

1.	TPNU	PUNT
2.	SNSEAO	SEASON
3.	IGLHTEILM	LIMELIGHT
4.	FREAV	FAVRE
5.	SUFMNRIO	UNIFORMS
6.	ADATENGVA	ADVANTAGE
7.	RUAGAJS	JAGUARS
8.	OESFRSIANPLO	PROFESSIONAL
9.	DEIIBLNSD	BLINDSIDE
10.	GHDILNO	HOLDING
11.	DSTROSIIUUN	INDUSTRIOUS
12.	RETFNECNIEER	INTERFERENCE
13.	ELHM	HELM
14.	RANMIO	MARINO
15.	UOTTCNINSRIS	INSTRUCTIONS
16.	OEBPDRITIH	PROHIBITED
17.	EANRTIR	TRAINER
18.	E94RS	49ERS
19.	PIGCPILN	CLIPPING
20.	IMLAECTOB	METABOLIC

Football Puzzle 9

106

1.	IINNAGTR	TRAINING
2.	DEPO	DOPE
3.	NIFYTRIELECG	ELECTRIFYING
4.	MOSS	MOSS
5.	DYRBA	BRADY
6.	RLUIUNGAA	INAUGURAL
7.	AITNST	TITANS
8.	SSTHLRUE	RUTHLESS
9.	UCTBIILYP	PUBLICITY
10.	GNIWINN	WINNING
11.	UEERSSRP	PRESSURE
12.	CEHLNOE	ECHELON
13.	LEIGLIBE	ELIGIBLE
14.	MANCEE	MENACE
15.	SEAGSIEGVR	AGGRESSIVE
16.	ERNAEUSMMET	MEASUREMENT
17.	RNNMITIIESOS	INTERMISSION
18.	ANMASTI	STAMINA
19.	OCUSROGUAE	COURAGEOUS
20.	ESND	ENDS

Football Puzzle 10

1.	AESMOWE	AWESOME
2.	WRIVAE	WAIVER
3.	NLF	NFL
4.	GENECPTAER	PERCENTAGE
5.	PAESSS	PASSES
6.	FDENOCIECN	CONFIDENCE
7.	LNEEISATP	PENALTIES
8.	TSRGINA	RATINGS
9.	MKAEROTW	TEAMWORK
10.	EVOCIEUNSTC	CONSECUTIVE
11.	EEISONILVT	TELEVISION
12.	ITVNAOO	OVATION
13.	KSCAERP	PACKERS
14.	NLUAUSU	UNUSUAL
15.	TNPREENVOI	PREVENTION
16.	EPSNRTAT	PATTERNS
17.	RAEG	GEAR
18.	FILOFAIC	OFFICIAL
19.	UITNGADN	DAUNTING
20.	ONONRINTCTFAO	CONFRONTATION

Football Puzzle 11

1. UHNSRGI   RUSHING

2. OENFESF   OFFENSE

3. AASDWR   AWARDS

4. EFRREEE   REFEREE

5. PITIOSON   POSITION

6. DNWO   DOWN

7. LLA-RSAT   ALL-STAR

8. ECDNNEAATT   ATTENDANCE

9. RIGETTNIY   INTEGRITY

10. EISDARR   RAIDERS

11. NSDNTEEMEOR   ENDORSEMENT

12. NSISTA   SAINTS

13. IUTSEPD   DISPUTE

14. ORTCTNAC   CONTRACT

15. SANF   FANS

16. GIAGZZ   ZIGZAG

17. ITMODANE   DOMINATE

18. INLSEDSEI   SIDELINES

19. AGDUR   GUARD

20. NIGAST   GIANTS

Football Puzzle 12

1. OWDRC   CROWD

2. OLUF   FOUL

3. PTO-AEDTR   TOP-RATED

4. OTCSU   SCOUT

5. ALYEW   ELWAY

6. PRVTONMEMEI   IMPROVEMENT

7. T-NATFROIOM   T-FORMATION

8. LLRO-UTO   ROLL-OUT

9. EERWITNVI   INTERVIEW

10. ODIVA   AVOID

11. ZNOE   ZONE

12. IOYRNETTO   NOTORIETY

13. ACMPTI   IMPACT

14. SEMSENI   NEMESIS

15. SPEDE   SPEED

16. SRGTTEAY   STRATEGY

17. EAAAPRCPEN   APPEARANCE

18. TERCEN   CENTER

19. AISUTN   UNITAS

20. IDAMNIRTOA   ADMIRATION

Football Puzzle 13

110

1. IKNARNG   RANKING

2. IOIAEMDCTN   MEDICATION

3. PSRTHAEN   PANTHERS

4. LBISL   BILLS

5. ISOLN   LIONS

6. AHOMNIPC   CHAMPION

7. AVNESR   RAVENS

8. SIEARP   PRAISE

9. AXEMIMIZ   MAXIMIZE

10. WNORB   BROWN

11. IDOSFEF   OFFSIDE

12. UOWHCTNDO   TOUCHDOWN

13. GRIT   GRIT

14. ANOYPT   PAYTON

15. RCAIERR   CARRIER

16. FTSHI   SHIFT

17. UHRS   RUSH

18. OCEPRTTONI   PROTECTION

19. ISNRSDKE   REDSKINS

20. OHYTU   YOUTH

Football Puzzle 14

111

1.	WSOOYBC	COWBOYS
2.	SSTO	TOSS
3.	LRVABULENE	VULNERABLE
4.	EEAGSL	EAGLES
5.	EADUBLI	AUDIBLE
6.	ETSJ	JETS
7.	ILPTS-OEDCSN	SPLIT-SECOND
8.	ORCDER	RECORD
9.	IOTLCNGEEERTLIA	INTERCOLLEGIATE
10.	TONANAM	MONTANA
11.	WRKUTOO	WORKOUT
12.	SOLBW	BOWLS
13.	SSCEULM	MUSCLES
14.	LUEDDH	HUDDLE
15.	CPCARTEI	PRACTICE
16.	BLRESCKO	BLOCKERS
17.	DAMARIG	DIAGRAM
18.	SMCIMEAGR	SCRIMMAGE
19.	ISYON	NOISY
20.	HTTWRA	THWART

Football Puzzle 15

1.	ERTNTAHE	THREATEN
2.	HSKAAWSE	SEAHAWKS
3.	LALC	CALL
4.	MAEMTTAE	TEAMMATE
5.	AGREAVE	AVERAGE
6.	CCHAO	COACH
7.	INCLIDPEIS	DISCIPLINE
8.	AEFM	FAME
9.	SOLS	LOSS
10.	DINW	WIND
11.	SYOFALFP	PLAYOFFS
12.	RWTOH	THROW
13.	GENERE	GREENE
14.	NCGIOSR	SCORING
15.	TAOTIRSP	PATRIOTS
16.	IEEFSVFNO	OFFENSIVE
17.	CFESHI	CHIEFS
18.	WLSIE	LEWIS
19.	GISALN	SIGNAL
20.	FESNITS	FITNESS

Football Puzzle 16

113

Made in the USA
Middletown, DE
22 December 2019

81686274R20071